AF604422

BE THE PERSON YOUR DOG THINKS YOU ARE

BE THE PERSON YOUR DOG THINKS YOU ARE

•••••••

C.J.FRICK

DRAWINGS BY LIZA DONNELLY

NERO

Published by Nero,
an imprint of Schwartz Publishing Pty Ltd
Level 1, 221 Drummond Street
Carlton VIC 3053, Australia
enquiries@blackincbooks.com
www.nerobooks.com

Illustrations by Liza Donnelly

First published by Flatiron Books,
an imprint of Macmillan Publishing Group
175 Fifth Avenue
New York, N.Y. 10010
www.flatironbooks.com

This edition published by arrangement with
Flatiron Books and is not for sale outside of ANZ.

9781760641023 (hardback)

A catalogue record for this book is available from the National Library of Australia

Cover design by Jen Clark
Cover illustrations by Liza Donnelly
Text design and typesetting by Steven Seighman

Printed in China by 1010 Printing International Limited.

To Oliver, who made me a better human every day

—LIZA DONNELLY

For Wally, the best dog there ever was

—C. J. FRICK

BE THE PERSON YOUR DOG THINKS YOU ARE

To be the person your dog thinks you are, you should…

Be affectionate.

prepare for the worst.

Be willing to burn the midnight oil.

Be wise enough to
walk away from conflict.

Get your hands dirty.

Be a team player.

Make time for what's really important.

Appreciate the little things.

Be generous.

Be spontaneous.

Be determined.

sit. –

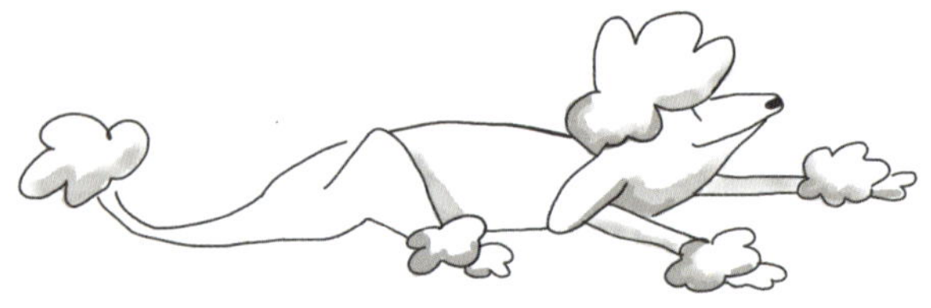

Teach with patience.

Celebrate special occasions.

HALLOWEEN
Princess

Exercise regularly.

Know when to break the rules.

Be brave.

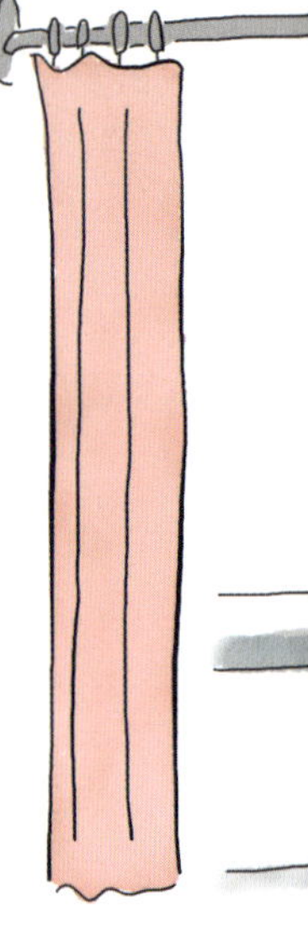

Appreciate the sacrifices of others.

Embrace the open road.

make new friends.

Be encouraging.

Be thankful for downtime.

Be the best part
of someone's day.

Be a friend for all seasons.

Forgive freely.

Protect the (adorably) fearful.

12
11
10
9
8
7
6

Respect routine.

Love nature.

Be part of your community.

Be charitable.

ANIMAL SHELTER

Be patient.

Expect the unexpected.

Keep an open mind.

Take the time to
make someone smile.

Lead with courage.

Be good in bed.

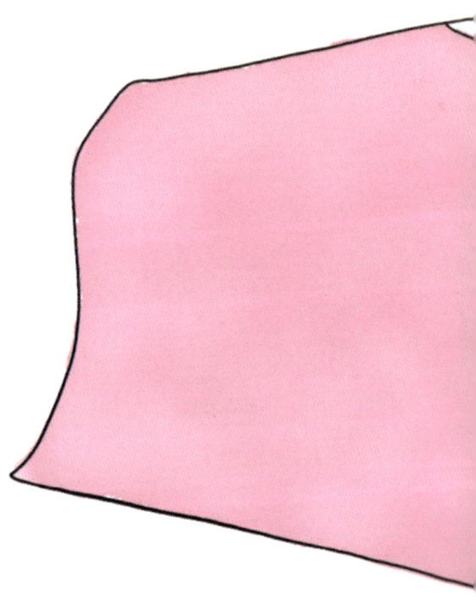

Be able to let loose.

understand that life

comes with messes.

Be gentle.

Be tough when required.

village
veterinarian

Embrace a lifelong commitment.

Be the person your dog
thinks you are.